How to

Get SSI & Social Security Disability

How to

Get SSI & Social Security Disability
Disability

An Insider's Step by Step Guide

Mike Davis

Writers Club Press
San Jose New York Lincoln Shanghai

How to Get SSI & Social Security Disability
An Insider's Step by Step Guide

Writers Club Press
an imprint of iUniverse.com, Inc.

For information address:
iUniverse.com, Inc.
620 North 48th Street, Suite 201
Lincoln, NE 68504-3467
www.iuniverse.com

DISCLAIMER—PLEASE READ CAREFULLY
The information contained in this book comes from the author's personal experience as a Disability Evaluation Analyst for the State of California. The intent is to assist SSI/SSA disability applicants to present a complete picture of their alleged physical and mental impairments. Since legislative and program changes occur frequently, the applicant is encouraged here, and throughout the book, to seek advice from the Social Security Administration and the Disability Determination Service of the state in which they reside. Legal advice from a competent attorney may also be appropriate. No guarantee or implied award of any kind is intended. No legal advice is offered herein.

ISBN: 0-595-12574-3

Printed in the United States of America

*T*o Dianne and Natalie, the two most important women in my life.

And God shall wipe away all tears from their eyes; and there shall be no more death, neither sorrow, nor crying, neither shall there be any more pain....

Revelation Chapter 21 verse 4
The Holy Bible

Contents

Part II: Increase Your Chances Even More

Preface

I have spent over seven years making determinations on SSI (Supplementary Security Income) and Social Security Disability claims for the State of California Department of Social Services, Disability and Adult Programs Division. I have worked on over 4,000 claims. I have spoken with hundreds of applicants (referred to as claimants), as well as attorneys, disability advocates, family members, physicians, medical record's clerks, psychologists, counselors, and many other people involved in the disability determination process.

Honestly, I have yet to meet anyone who does not work directly in the field as a Disability Examiner or Medical Consultant who knows what is needed to give a claimant the best chance of being allowed disability benefits. In fact, most of us in the field have had to deny claims when we truly believed the person was probably disabled. However, the evidence was just not complete enough to make a favorable decision(I'll say more about this later). The purpose of this book is to explain how a claimant, child or adult, physically and/or mentally impaired, can truthfully and legally maximize the possibility of being successful in an attempt to be found disabled. I don't know any other one-stop place that you can get this information in simple step by step language.

If you have a family member or friend who is applying for disability, this will be an especially valuable guide. Often the person applying for disability needs help from someone else due to the mental and physical limitations they have. For a healthy, mentally alert individual, the process is challenging. For someone who is ill, in pain and confused, it becomes monumental. This book can help the helpers, including the professionals who serve as advocates and representatives. Here is a map of the maze so you can help others find their way.

Another group of claimants who will benefit from this book are those who are currently receiving SSI or Social Security Disability. Every one to seven years congress has mandated that disability claims be reviewed to see if the claimant is still unable to work. These are called Continuing Disability Reviews (CDR). While the standard of review is a little different than that used for the first time claim, generally the same standards for disability apply to both the new and continuing case review. The information in this book can help those on disability prepare for the review process and insure that the best case possible will be presented to keep their benefits coming.

This is not a long book. Over and over I found myself tempted to make it longer and include more information; but when I asked myself if an applicant really needed the additional information, I had to answer no. Although the process and technicalities are professionally interesting to me, I tried to keep in mind the reader and keep it as simple as possible. The book is divided into two parts.

Part I takes a checklist approach and gives practical step by step directions from filling out the application to final decision. I have purposely kept this part brief and simple. Let's face it, some of this stuff is next to impossible to understand and not even the Social Security Disability experts can agree on what it means. Part I may be all you want or need. It will get you through the necessary steps quickly and yet thoroughly.

Part II gives a more detailed overview of the entire process and includes important information that many will want to read after or while completing the steps in part I. Here you'll find invaluable tips and insights about how to work within, and navigate through, the system of Social Security Disability. Knowing who the players are in the system and what each one has that you need to get for your claim is of major importance. Alienating any of those players can hurt you. This is a very human process, and there are many people that you need on your side. I will give you my "take" on how to get the most out of everyone involved, so that your chances rise dramatically for a favorable allowance.

Keep in mind that recent statistics, informally reported at my California office, have shown that only 30% of initial claims are allowed; however, at the appeals level, 70% of claims are allowed, meaning many initial decisions are reversed. Social Security has been trying to implement more standardized processes so that more cases are allowed initially. How successful that will be is unknown. We do know that appeals can add months or years of time waiting for a decision. Getting it right the first time is our goal.

I have included several appendices for your use to track information that is needed for your claim and make important notes. I have also purposely repeated myself at several places and on several points. Not everyone needs to read every word of every section, although I would encourage you to do so. Repetition reinforces key points and shows you what I consider to be important enough to be repeated. If you find yourself saying I already got that, make sure you did get it and that you took action on that point.

I have used the largest print(font)practicable in a book of this size, knowing that many readers will be elderly and some will have visual impairments.

Acknowledgments

I gratefully acknowledge the training and support I received from Cynthia Mejia, Katharine Gray, and Gay Tanner: each unique in temperament and talent; each a consummate professional.

List of Abbreviations

See the glossary for definitions

ADL—Activities of Daily Living
ALJ—Administrative Law Judge
CDR—Continuing Disability Review
CE—Consultative Examination
CR—Claims Representative
DDS—Disability Determination Service
DE—Disability Examiner
DEA—Disability Evaluation Analyst
FO—Field Office
MC—Medical Consultant
MSS—Medical Source Statement
RECON—Reconsideration
SSA—Social Security Administration

Introduction

Introduction to the Disability Process

There is just no way to avoid giving you details that may be tedious and somewhat confusing. Hopefully this overview will make what follows clearer.

Social Security does not make the **medical decision** about whether you are disabled or not; they have given that job to the individual states. Each state has an agency for just that purpose. The federal government calls these agencies the Disability Determination Service (DDS). In California the state Department of Social Services has a division dedicated to making disability determinations. Other states may give the responsibility to another agency. Each state, however, uses the same laws, rules and regulations mandated by the United States Congress. Regardless of the state where you reside and what agency is designated to make the decision, the rules are federal rules and are the same everywhere. The information in this book is valid in any place where you are eligible to apply for SSI or Social Security Disability. The local Social Security Office will determine if you meet the **administrative rules** for eligibility for either SSI or Social Security Disability or both.

A Disability Examiner (DE), working with a Medical Consultant (MC), makes the medical decision about whether you can work or not, and thus whether or not you are eligible medically for disability. Each state has separate titles for the Examiner; in California they are called Disability Evaluation Analysts.

Local Social Security Offices take initial applications from applicants, who are referred to as claimants. The person who takes the application is called a Claim's Representative (CR). The local Social Security Office is referred to as the Field Office (FO). Social Security at the federal level is referred to as the Social Security Administration (SSA). As you read have faith that the abbreviations will begin to make sense. The CR at the FO makes all the **administrative** decisions regarding the claimants eligibility for disability. That is, citizenship, enough work history, financial eligibility, when payments start and how much they will be, etc. The administrative issues of eligibility cannot be argued or influenced much; however, there is a great deal of discretion and personal judgment involved in the medical decision. This book will help you provide the necessary information so that the DE and MC can accurately determine if you are disabled or not.

We will be using abbreviations throughout this book, starting with those noted above, and use for the most part the federal terminology. You will encounter some differences from state to state, but everyone should understand the federal terminology. I will define each term the first time it is used and then include it in a list of abbreviations for reference. You may want to make a copy of this and have it in front of you to refer to as you read.

Also you will note that I use **he** and **him** most of the time in this book. I intend it to be understood in the generic sense of persons of any gender, human beings, male and female, and use it only for the sake of convenience and stylistic consistency.

PART I

Step by Step Instructions

Introduction to Part I

In this section I will be as brief as possible and still give you what you absolutely must do. At times it may look like cookbook language; here I want to provide you with a bare-bones recipe that includes most of what you need to know and do. In this section your best bet is just to take my advice and do what I recommend (unless someone from Social Security or the DDS tells you something different. You must always follow their instructions). Later I will give you the reasons why, but for now please take my word that every single thing I am asking you to do is very important to your claim. Nothing is here that is just paperwork or busywork.

It is also important to note that there is no **recipe** for a disability claim. The evaluation of each claim is as varied and complex as any medical impairment might be. One of the buzz-words Disability Examiners here over and over is that each claim is determined on a "case by case basis," meaning that individual judgment is required. Each case is slightly different. However, the elements needed to make that decision are the same, as we'll repeat over and over. Those elements are the medical, nonmedical, and vocational evidence necessary for the DE and MC to accurately determine if a claimant is disabled or not, according to Social Security rules.

CHAPTER 1

The Application

Introduction

The first rule for the application is **completeness**. Many applications are incomplete and the Disability Examiner (DE) may or may not have the time, energy, or initiative to contact the claimant to get what is needed. It is the responsibility of the **claimant** to provide accurate and complete information. If you don't put it down, it may never get looked at and will not be part of the information considered in determining your claim.

We will assume you have in front of you a Social Security Disability Application. Use the instructions below to help make it as complete as possible. Some of you may not have gotten this book until after you filed an application for disability. You can still use the information here. If you see areas where you need to revise or include more information you can simply write it down and **make a copy**, sign it, date it, and send it to the Disability Examiner working on your case. A hand written note that is legible is fine; just say something like here is some more information I would like to include for my case. **Include your Social Security number on all correspondence.** If in doubt about anything, call the DE and he will tell you what you need to do.

If your claim is still at the FO (the local Social Security Office) and has not yet been sent to the DDS (the state agency that makes the medical decision), you may be able to make changes over the phone with the CR (the Claims Representative at the local Social Security Office) handling your case. Call the FO and ask them if the case has gone to the DDS, and if so get the telephone number and name of the DE (Disability Examiner) who is handling your claim. Call the DE, collect is fine for long distance, and get the correct address and let him know over the phone what updates you are sending.

As a general rule: Once your claim has been sent to the DDS do not send any information to the FO to forward to the DDS. There is a very good chance we at the DDS will never get it. It may seem that you are making things happen more quickly or that you are helping by taking a form in person or hand-carrying it to the FO, but in reality you are delaying your claim. Now it has to be handled by the person at the desk at the Social Security Office, who must get it to the right CR. The CR must find out who the DE is who is handling your claim and then mail or courier it to him. Most claimants do not understand that the DE working on your case may be in an office hundreds of miles away. Papers given to the FO have an uncanny way of getting lost in the mail or the office. I have visited the local Social Security Office and to say that the Claim's Reps are overworked is an understatement. They have a tough job and 1000's of claims pass through their hands. Things get lost at both the federal and state offices. Send what you have straight to the DE at the state office unless you have some compelling reason to do otherwise. This will increase your odds of not having it get lost. Of course, anything the FO has requested should never be sent to the DDS/DE either. That could just as easily disappear and not reach the FO/CR. Now to the steps.

The Application Step by Step

Step 1. Call your local Social Security Office and tell them you want to apply for disability. Some sort of arrangement will be made for you to apply over the telephone or go to the office for a face to face interview. Whatever the arrangement you should ask that the application be mailed to you to complete prior to your phone or in person appointment. With your application will come a letter that lists all the documents you must provide to Social Security, like birth certificates, alien cards, Social Security numbers, etc. Be sure you get copies of all these for the Claims Rep prior to your meeting or to mail in with your application.

Step 2. Answer every question on the application. If you do not understand one or more of the questions, call the Social Security Office (FO) and ask for help.

Step 3. Be sure to list every illness that contributes to your inability to work, **physical and mental.** Has your heart attack caused you to be depressed? List it. If you don't know the names of your illnesses, then describe them in sufficient detail for the DE to understand how your illnesses limit your ability to work.

Step 4. List **every** treating source; that is, every doctor or medical professional that treated you. Give complete addresses, zip codes, and telephone numbers with area codes. Include those treating sources that you saw for at least two years before you became disabled. Disability Examiners (DEs) must have a longitudinal record (history) of the progression of your illnesses. In the appropriate section be sure to include any information regarding tests, x-rays, etc. Attach additional sheets of paper if the application does not provide enough space to list them all.

Step 5. List another person or two in the third-party contact section that can be reached if the Disability Examiner cannot reach you. Give complete name, address, zip, telephone number with area code, and relationship. It would probably be a good idea to contact these people and let them know that you have listed them on your application.

Step 6. In the section on work information, give **complete** answers to the questions about how much you lifted, how long each work day you stood or sat, how often you had to stoop or bend, etc. **This section refers to what you did on your job, not what you can do now.** Often claimants misunderstand this section and put down answers like, "I can't lift anything." The Examiner must then send out another form or make a call to clarify the answer. **Be sure you give a complete 15-year work history.** This means 15 years prior to when you quit working or you are alleging that you became disabled. For instance, if you are applying for disability in July of 2000, but you are alleging you have been disabled since September of 1996, you need to provide a complete work history for the 15 years prior to September of 1996, not from January of 2000. If you have done any work **since** you became disabled, you need to give complete details about those jobs too, especially if you tried to work but were unable to continue because you were too ill.

For at least the last employer give the correct and full name of the company, address and zip, telephone and contact person. The examiner may want to send the employer a form to fill out that can verify the worsening of your illness or your inability to work.

Step 7. Children's Claims: For children's claims, the equivalent of work history is school history. Give complete addresses with zip codes, and telephone numbers with area codes, for all the schools your child attended, including day-care, Head-Start programs, etc. In the section on baby-sitters and day-care providers do the same. Normally schools that have been attended during the last two years are sufficient, but if you care to list schools going further back it is okay. Most important is the current school that has your child's records and knows him well enough to provide information on his functioning at school.

Step 8. You may or may not be given supplementary questionnaires to fill out by the CR. The most common would be the Daily Activities Questionnaire (ADL for Activities of Daily Living). Most questionnaires will come directly from the DDS and DE; however, some CRs try to be helpful and knowing that the claim will require the form, they will provide it at the interview or send it with the application. For children it may be called a Supplementary Function Questionnaire or Form. Here just note, these are **very** important. Be complete; much of your claim may hinge on your answers here. **Make copies of everything you send to the FO. Trust me, your chances of having something lost are very high** (as we noted above). It's surprising how well the Field Offices keep track of what they do with their limited resources and the workload they have. That's not your problem, but it will be your problem if something is lost and you haven't made a copy of it.

Step 9. If your address or telephone number changes, call both the Social Security Office (FO) and the Disability Examiner (DE) with the new information. **Never count on Social Security to pass the information on to the Examiner.** Any correspondence from the Examiner will have his telephone number and address on it. If you lose his name, address, or telephone number, you can always call Social Security and they should be able to tell you who the Examiner working on your case is, or give you a number to call to find out.

Step 10. Remember you have the right to talk to a supervisor any time you feel you can't get a response that is reasonable or useful from either a Social Security Claims Representative (CR) or a Disability Examiner (DE). If you get no satisfaction from the supervisor, ask for the next supervisor up. You can also contact your federal Congressional Representative and ask him or her to intervene on your behalf. This has some limited value, but I would exhaust every local remedy first. It may get the attention of the DE, but after all, there is really only so much anyone can do to a DE to get him working harder, when he's already working overtime and giving it all he can. There are limitations that no threat is going to be able to overcome. Maintaining the best relationship you can with the DE will do the most for you. When legitimate abuses occur, however, you should be aware that you do have recourse to the options listed above.

Step 11. Be **truthful** on your application. All sorts of red flags go up and your credibility begins to erode if the Examiner finds repeated discrepancies, inconsistencies, and contradictions in the information you provide. Of course, you can only do your best, and most Examiners aren't looking for little errors or lapses in memory. They do, however, develop a sense of what begins to look like a pattern of misleading statements that appear to be given to bolster a claim. You, of course, do not need to be reminded that it is a crime to make fraudulent statements on your application and that you may be imprisoned, fined, or both if you are guilty of such crimes.

Step 12. Call the CR at the FO and ask for a status on your claim and find out if there is anything else you need to do, or if there is any way you can help him?

CHAPTER 2

The Disability
Determination Service

Introduction

As we have said, Disability Determination Service (DDS) is the name given by Social Security (SSA) to the State Agency that makes the decision as to whether or not a claimant is disabled. Disability Examiner (DE) is the federal title of the person who is a state employee and actually makes the medical decision. The local Social Security Office is known as the Field Office (FO).

Once your application has been processed at the FO it is sent to the DDS where it is assigned to a DE. Your medical records are requested using the sources you provided on your application and the medical releases you signed at the FO. You very likely will receive more questionnaires to fill out in the mail from the DE. Many of the forms will be produced locally, that is they will not be federal forms. Some of the more common forms are: asthma, HIV, pain, seizure,

Activities of Daily Living (mainly for mental impairments), Exertional Daily Activities (usually used in heart and some other physical impairments), fatigue, and others depending on the office at which your claim is being processed and what your alleged impairments are. Records from schools, questionnaires to employers, tests from psychologists, and many other items will be gathered. As soon as the DE believes he has a complete enough picture to determine your capacity for work, he summarizes his findings, makes a recommendation, and sends your case to the Medical Consultant (MC).

The MC may be a physical doctor, medical specialist, psychiatrist, or Ph.D. licensed clinical psychologist. He will give an opinion, based on all the information and using the DE's summary and recommendation, as to what, if any, physical and/or mental limitations exist that would limit your work activities. Using this assessment, the DE will then do a vocational analysis, using the descriptions and job titles of past work that you have provided, to see if you are deemed capable of working.

An estimate of how long the entire process will take is very difficult to give you. In California, we at the DDS, tried to get a case finished on average within 60 days or so. How long it took to get to us from the FO is another question. Some cases I have done in one day because the case came with medical records and it was a clear-cut allowance. These are usually terminal cases and some others that are well defined. Other cases took months. I think you are looking at several months on average. It may seem like I have not answered the question, "How Long?" The problem in making an estimate is that every case is different. If you call the DE you will often get answers like, "It all depends." On what you'll ask? Then the DE will go into a litany of whether your doctor responds timely, if his records are sufficient and on and on it goes. From the claimants standpoint I think a fair answer to the question is "a long time-too long." You can be assured though, that the DE is under great pressure to finish your case as quickly as possible. Delays will often upset him, especially the delays caused by the claimant, for example not showing up for a Consultative Examination, not providing all the information in the application for medical sources and impairments, or failing to call with address changes.

This is a very complex process, and I have so simplified it here that DEs and MCs everywhere will criticize this description. I will though, in keeping with our step by step approach in Part 1, leave it at that and provide further detail in Part 2. Having said that, I must warn you that this chapter is much more complicated than Chapter 1. Each step has multiple parts to it and does not lend itself easily to a numbered step by step approach. Therefore we will approach it topically and put several steps together under each topic. This is the heart of your disability claim, and what you do with this information will have a large bearing on the decision that is rendered by the DDS and DE.

Medical Records: The Heart of Your Claim

MEDICAL RECORDS: Getting your medical records is a major priority for the DE and the most important evidence in your file. There are several snags that can occur here and there are many things you can do to insure that as complete a medical picture as possible is provided to the DE and MC. If you do not have any medical records or if they are insufficient to determine whether or not you are disabled, you may be required to go to a medical examination (Consultative Medical Examination, CE) arranged and paid for by DDS/SSA. We will say more about this later.

Step 1. Make sure you have provided the DE with all your treating sources (doctors, counselors, social workers, hospitals, labs, tests done, etc.).

Step 2. If you have seen any new treating sources since you filed your application, call the DE and give that information to him so he can request those records.

Step 3. If you have any severe new illnesses or injuries since your claim was filed notify the DE. I would define severe to mean any illnesses that limit your function or ability to work.

Step 4. If any major treatments, especially surgeries, have been done or are scheduled to be done since you filed your claim, notify the DE.

Step 5. Notify the DE if any of your illnesses have gotten significantly worse since you filed your claim. I would define significant to mean "quite a bit worse." Use your common sense.

Step 6. Call your treating sources and make sure your records have been requested and that they have sent them to the DE. Two to three weeks is an average time for a treating source to respond; a month is too long for the average DE and he is getting a bit anxious about things-leading to the next step.

Step 7. Call the DE and find out what treating sources are not responding to his requests so you can contact them and gently encourage them to help you by sending the records.

Step 8. Get copies of your records yourself and send **copies** directly to the DE if your treating source(s) are not responding timely. The DE will tell you if you need to intervene.

Step 9. Call the DE and ask for a status on your claim and find out if there is anything else needed and if there is anything you can do to help. Calling once every couple weeks and letting the DE know that you are willing to do whatever you can to help is not out of line.

✦✦✦

Medical Source Statement: The Determining Factor

Medical Source Statement: This is often **the determining factor as to whether you will be found disabled or not.** The Medical Source Statement (MSS) is your doctor's opinion about what work related activity you can do. He must support his opinion with medical evidence in the form of physical or mental exams, lab reports, history and other medical information (more about this later). His opinions must be stated in a form that is acceptable to SSA. The easiest way to accomplish this is to use an MSS form that the DE can provide to you. If you have a treating physician get an MSS from him.

Step 1. Call the DE and ask him to send you a blank MSS form. If you are alleging a mental illness you will need a mental MSS form, and a physical MSS form for a physical allegation. If you have mental and physical illnesses get both and send them to both your physical and mental doctors. Ask the DE to send you return envelopes for each form. **Be sure you always put the name of the DE on the return envelope.** In a big office it can take an extra day or two to route mail that isn't sent to the attention of the DE. First the mail has to be opened and searched for the claimant's name. Then it has to be queried on a computer or some other way to find who the DE is who is handling this claimant's case. This may not be a priority for the mail room that gets 100's and sometimes 1000's of pieces of mail a day. Remember, in the office I was in, there were 10,000 or more active claims at any given time.

Step 2. Make copies of the **blank MSS** form(s) in case they are lost at your doctor's office or at the DDS. You don't want to have to call the DE for another form because it was lost. This will slow your claim and also make more work for an already overworked and harried DE.

Step 3. Mail or hand-carry the form(s) to your doctor(s) and request that they be completed and returned in the return envelope(s). Let him know how important this is. **It is difficult to overstate the importance of your doctor's input.**

Step 4. Follow-up with the DE to see if he has received the MSS yet. Once a week is about often enough. Anymore often and you risk becoming a nuisance.

Step 5. Follow-up with your doctor and encourage him to complete the MSS. Ten (10) to fourteen (14) days is not an unreasonable time for your doctor to complete the MSS for you, although your doctor might disagree with this time frame. Gentle pressure and persuasion is what is needed. Courtesy and thank yous are always in order.

Step 6. Stay in touch with both your doctor and DE and ask if there is anything you can do to help them with your case?

***

Physical and Mental Examinations

An MSS without a current physical exam or mental status exam is insufficient. If your doctor does not, will not, or cannot provide a current mental and/or physical exam, then the DE will have to purchase a Consultative Examination. **The more information your own doctor provides the better.** Who knows your condition better: the doctor who has been treating you over a period of time or a doctor who has seen you once for 15 to 30 minutes? The importance of your own doctor's participation in your examinations should be obvious.

Step 1. Find out from your doctor if he has included a recent exam (physical and/or mental) in your records? Recent means within the last **60 days for a mental status exam** and within the last **six months for a physical exam.**

Step 2. Call the DE and find out if he got an exam with your records, and if it was complete enough to make a decision; most often the exam is not complete enough for the DE, so don't assume anything. Make the call and find out. If it is not complete enough, **ask the DE to send you a form for your doctor to fill out for a physical and/or mental exam.** Don't just go to your doctor and ask for an exam; nine times out of ten the exam he does will miss items the DE is required to have. **Don't mistake a follow-up appointment with your doctor for an examination.** We mean a full physical or mental exam.

Step 3. Call your doctor and arrange an appointment for an exam, explaining that Social Security Disability is requiring you to get the exam. If you do not have insurance and the doctor wants to charge for the exam, call the DE and ask how much SSA will pay and make arrangements to have the doctor paid directly by the DE. Even if you do have insurance, SSA/DDS will pay for the examination, if SSA/DDS requires that you have an examination for purposes of making a disability determination.

Step 4. Be sure your doctor has the address and the name of the DE to whom the completed examination should be directed. Emphasize to him that your disability claim is on hold until he sends in the exam.

Step 5. Follow-up with both the DE and your physician to make sure the MSS and physical/mental exam were received and are sufficient for a decision.

Step 6. If asked at any point during the disability process to attend an examination, have testing done, or any other requirement, do it. **Failure to do so can result in an automatic disqualification.** You can be reimbursed for mileage, provided with bus tickets and in some instances even a taxi to get to the examination.

Step 7. This point should be obvious by now: **Stay in touch with the DE and ask if there is anything you need to do or can do to help with your claim?**

***

Questionnaires: More Important Than You Think

Questionnaires: We have mentioned questionnaires above briefly, but they are so important that we must now go into more detail. You will get a number of questionnaires and forms from the Disability Examiner. Most of them will be forms about your medical problems, exertional limitations (what you can and cannot do), and your work history. Although many of these will be filled out by sources other than doctors and are technically not medical evidence, they are **very** important. This is not just busy work. Remember the Examiner usually sends out the minimum he can get by with. He is overworked and pushed to move cases, so whatever you get is vital to your case. Some of the forms are titled "third party." This means that someone other than the claimant needs to fill out this form.

A Family member or anyone who knows you well is fine for third party forms. A call I most often get is to ask if family members can fill out third party forms. The answer is yes, unless some special person like a teacher or day-care worker is indicated. If you have no other person who knows you well enough to fill out the third party form, write on the front of the form, "I have no third party to complete this from," and return it. You should not be penalized for that and returning the questionnaire with that information keeps your file complete.

Take great care with these forms. Sometimes these questionnaires can tip the scales one way or the other. Be prompt returning them. Cases sometimes are ready to have a decision made and sit waiting for a claimant form to be returned. Occasionally a claim is be denied for insufficient evidence because a claimant would not return a questionnaire and the evidence in the file is incomplete. The claim is denied for lack of cooperation.

If you receive any questionnaires from the Social Security Office to fill out, **make copies.** Very often in the office where I worked I had to have duplicate forms completed by claimants, both adults and children, because they were lost somewhere between the Social Security Field Office and the Disability Determination Service office where the Examiner works. Be forewarned. Some examples of forms would be Activities of Daily Living; Pain Questionnaire; Asthma Questionnaire; Child's Function Report, and many, many, more.

The examiner cannot make a determination without this information, so if you get a call from the DE or a form in the mail, even though you already filled out this same form, it won't do you any good as a claimant to get angry. This can be very frustrating for claimants, but the Examiner doesn't have it or he would not be asking for it. If you have a copy send it. If you didn't make a copy, fill it out again, make a copy and mail it in. This is another time to be reminded that alienating decision makers is not in your best interest. Is your goal to win an argument or get your claim processed quickly and accurately? Even if you walk away feeling like, "I really let him have a piece of my mind," you are still going to have fill out the form, so what did you really accomplish?

I recommend making copies of everything you send to anyone, at any office, involved in the disability process. This becomes even more important if your claim is denied and you appeal the decision. It would not be a bad idea to also keep a log of all your telephone calls, noting the date, number, and person you called, along with the subject and content of the call. I have provided simple record keeping sheets in the appendixes for this purpose. This too could be invaluable at the appeals level or if it becomes necessary to get an attorney. Note when you called and left messages and whether or not the call was ever returned. Most DEs return calls, but not all do. Document as much of the process as you can.

∗∗∗

Exit Interview or Reconsideration?

The Exit Interview: At the time of this writing the disability process is undergoing redesign nation wide. Whether this will be continued in subsequent administrations is anybody's guess. During my seven years I have seen many so-called changes come and go at both the federal and state levels. It is best to be prepared. The major change being made at the time of this writing is that prior to a claim being denied the claimant will have a chance to respond in writing, by telephone, or in person with any additional information he wants included in the decision. You may be notified by mail or telephone. There will surely be deadlines, probably something along the lines of from three to ten days. **Be Prepared.**

If you get that call or letter, find out from the DE if all your medical sources were indeed received? Was an MSS received? Did the DE receive all the questionnaires you mailed? In short, go over all that you have done and make sure everything you wanted included was considered. If not, you should be given the opportunity to submit anything else that is relevant to your claim. If you have had any new illnesses, treatments, or worsening of your condition since your last contact, this is the time to indicate that. This is your last chance before your case goes to the appeal level, which very likely will take at least several months to a year or more unless some radical changes have taken place by the time you are reading this.

Step 1. Be prepared for a call or letter that your claim has been denied. Remember, at my branch there was an informal statistic that indicated about 70% of all initial claims were denied. That means you have a better than 2 out of 3 chance of getting that call or letter. **Prepare now for the call. Prepare your records and papers so you can check to be sure your claim has been developed thoroughly and everything you wanted in your claim is there. Prepare psychologically, so you are not shocked when you get a denial call. Expect it.**

Step 2. During the call or if there is a face to face interview option and you choose to do that, ask the DE if there is anything you can do to strengthen your claim. The DE is the real expert. This is where you can get the inside story on what's going on. You just might find out that your claim is very close to being an allowance but lacks something that you can provide. If so, find out what it is and see if you can get it. **Write it down.** Don't trust your memory. The DE may have some very specific piece of evidence he needs. I wouldn't argue or become abusive with the DE, this cannot help you. Instead ask for help. What more can I do? Is there anything else you can recommend? If this were your own claim what would you do now? Listen very carefully to the DEs answers to your questions. Telling the DE why you should be found disabled is generally not very productive. The DE can only make decisions based on evidence.

***

One last piece of business here.

You'll note our subject head mentioned something called a reconsideration. The reconsideration is scheduled to be deleted and replaced by the exit interview at denial. However, at this time some cases are still being reconsidered at denial, as the exit interview is being phased in, and DEs are being trained. A reconsideration is just a second look at the claim by another DE and MC. You, the claimant, must apply for the reconsideration and submit any new evidence you want considered. There is more information on reconsiderations in Part II.

***

Children's Claims: Difficult At Best

Children's Claims: One of the most important pieces of evidence in claims for children of school age is the Teacher Questionnaire. The DE will send a request to your child's school for his records, testing results, and other information. In addition, a Teacher Questionnaire will be enclosed to be forwarded to your child's teacher for observations on learning, behavior, and other issues. These are mailed directly to the school or district office.

Often the Teacher Questionnaire is not forwarded to the teacher by the school office staff or school district staff; or it is sent to a teacher who is not the best informed person to comment on your child's functioning. It could be sent to a teacher who does not see this form as a priority. **A school age child's claim can seldom be determined without the teacher's observations.**

I suggest if at all possible you call the Disability Examiner who is handling your child's case and ask that, in addition to his mailing the Teacher Questionnaire directly to the school, he would also send you a blank form with a return envelope. You can then take the form directly to the teacher that knows your child best. Take the Teacher Questionnaire in person to the teacher if possible and kindly ask that it be fully completed and returned quickly. Remember, this is one of those people you want on your side. Be nice. In addition to being able to choose the teacher best suited to assess your child, the questionnaire will likely be completed with more care and returned more quickly, when the teacher understands how important this is to you.

Something you should make clear to the teacher, even though it is stated on the Teacher Questionnaire, is that the questions regarding how your child functions are in comparison to a normal child. Some teachers in special education classes will indicate that a child is doing well, but he is comparing the child to a group of disabled children. The DE needs to know how the child functions compared to the normal school aged child in his peer group. I have had teachers tell me a child was a high achiever in his class only to find out that the most severely disabled children were in his class, and the "high achiever" was more than 50% behind his peers in the mainstream of the school. This is another good reason to take the form in person to the teacher if you can.

Another problem is that schools often just don't respond to requests for records. In the summer or over vacations most often there is no one working in the school office and the request may sit for literally months. **You must intervene with the school if you want a reasonable chance of getting a full picture of your child's illnesses in the record or avoiding months of delay .**

Step 1. Call the DE and ask to have a copy of the Teacher Questionnaire form sent to you with a return envelope. Be sure the name of the DE is on the envelope.

Step 2. If at all possible, hand carry the Teacher Questionnaire, with a return envelope, to the teacher who knows your child's problems best, and ask him to complete and return it. Emphasize how important his assessment is and thank him for his effort.

Step 3. Call the school and verify that a request for your child's school records, including testing, and speech and language reports, have been received. Verify that they have been sent to the DE or ask for the date they are expected to be sent so you can follow-up on this. Get the name of the person with whom you are speaking.

Step 4. Follow-up on all elements of the information needed from the school. Remember that many of the items come from different offices. You will have to find out from the school where each piece is coming from. For each service your child receives there may be a different person who is responsible for mailing records: School psychologist, principal for behavior problems, speech and language specialist, learning and reading problems specialist, etc.

Step 5. Though not a separate step, recognize that children's claims are considered by most DEs to be the most difficult claims to adjudicate (determine) because of the volume of evidence needed and the difficulty in getting it. In addition, the complexity of human development at various ages requires a great deal of knowledge on the part of the DE and MC. Ask the DE for a list of every piece of school information he is after and then aggressively pursue that information.

All the other general steps listed previously also apply to children's claims.

✦✦✦

Children's Function Questionnaires:

This is the child equivalent of the adult Daily Activities Questionnaire (ADL). Without this form it is likely no decision can be reached on a child claim. This is sent to the parent, guardian, care-giver, group home or institution where the child is being cared for. As we noted above this is another critical piece of evidence. **Take your time and answer every question as completely as possible.**

Step 1. Make sure you received a function questionnaire from the DE. If not, call and have one sent with a return envelope immediately.

Step 2. Functional Questionnaires are divided by age groups (e.g. birth to 12 months; 1 year to 3 years old; and so on through age 16. At age 16 an adult questionnaire is appropriate). Make sure the form you got is for the correct age of your child. If there are questions that make no sense to you, for instance your child is 5 months old and a question asks what kind of work he does, this is a clue that you have the wrong form. Call and get the age appropriate form.

Step 3. Can you guess this one? **Make a copy of the completed form.** This is a long and complex form. If it gets lost you don't want to do it again. Mail it in the return envelope to the DE.

Step 4. About a week later call the DE and ask if he received the form and if it is complete enough. The functional form often raises new issues and the DE may have questions for you that may lead to new testing that is needed or clarification from your doctor. This is a good time to see where you stand in the process.

✶✶✶

Read This Important Hint:

I considered leaving this for Part II, but I don't want to risk anyone missing this vital information. When I was an analyst (DE) and was called by a claimant asking if everything that was needed was in, I routinely told him that if I needed anything additional I would call him. In other words stop calling me and let me do the work; and I did follow-up. However, not every DE will call you, or something may just be inadvertently overlooked. No one cares about your claim more than you do and you must take responsibility for it. Calling any more than about once a week and you risk being viewed as a nuisance and may alienate the DE (the last thing you want to happen). Group some of the questions and topics together and try to do them with one call instead of calling every day or two with a new question.

You'll need to play this by ear and try to read the DE and what's going on with him. Be very courteous, even if he is curt. Remember the supervisor can be contacted as noted above, but try to work with DE. The DE has great discretionary power and although nearly all those I have worked with have tried to be objective and fair, it can't hurt to have a friend in this position. I'm not saying you won't get a fair decision, just that all the factors involved in any human interaction are involved in this transaction. I hope I've made my point here.

✳✳✳

Help, I Don't Have A Doctor:

Many claimants do not have doctors. If this is your case, you will be asked to attend a Consultative Examination (CE). You may have to see several doctors, a psychiatrist, a physical specialist, a psychologist for mental testing, get lab tests or other kinds of medical testing. These will all be paid for by SSA and the examining physician will do an MSS for you. These doctors do not work for Social Security or the state. However, some do work for companies that specialize in doing exams for disability claims, and a common complaint is that exams are not as complete as the claimant would have liked. **You must make known to the doctor your history, illnesses, complaints, limitations and anything else that limits your ability to work. Make him listen to you.**

Tell the doctor what you can and cannot do in terms that he can quantify: I cannot stand for more than 15 minutes without severe pain; I cannot lift more than 10 pounds repeatedly; I cannot bend over; I can't complete a task I start; I become confused easily; I can't sleep, etc. I hope you realize that these are just examples of numbers of different limitations you have and not suggestions. Be truthful and give an accurate account of your limitations or an honest estimate if you are not sure. Be sure to include items not easily measured such as pain and fatigue. If you do not tell the doctor what your limitations are he may infer from the examination that you can do more than you really can. On the other hand you should know that doctors are experts at spotting exaggerations of symptoms and there are special tests and observations to determine if a patient is exaggerating. **Truthfulness and honesty** are always best.

PART II

Increase Your Chances Even More

Introduction to Part II

Your chances for a favorable determination can be increased by understanding in more depth some of the items we have already covered, as well as getting some knowledge of areas we have not yet touched on. This section will benefit everyone, but strictly speaking Part I covered the absolute heart of the disability process. I would like to encourage you to read all of Part II. You may, however, benefit from scanning the sections and identifying those topics which are especially important and pertinent to your situation.

CHAPTER 3

More on Medical Records, Exams and the MSS.

Unfortunately it is not always a priority for your doctor to respond to the letter the DDS sends him asking for your medical records to be sent to the DE. You can help by calling your doctor and letting him or her know that a request is on the way and that it be handled in a timely fashion. The DE should contact you, the claimant, if vital medical information is not received, but you cannot always count on that. In fact I would count on that not happening. I would suggest that about two weeks after medical requests have been mailed to your treating sources you call the DE and find out what records have not been received (you know it's been 2 weeks because that's how long ago you got your questionnaires, which were probably mailed out at the same time as the requests for your medical records. If you haven't gotten any questionnaires or forms to fill out, and some claimants don't because not every impairment requires a special form, then you should call the DE and find out when the requests for medical records were mailed).

Call your doctors who have not responded, and courteously ask them when they expect to send the records to the DDS? If after a month, from the time the original request was mailed, the doctor still has not responded, I would suggest that you request a complete copy of your records from the physician, to which you are legally entitled. **Make copies** of all your records and forward them to the DE. **Call the DE** and tell him they are on the way. Check back with the DE to make sure they were received.

Your doctor may charge you a copying or office fee for this. Call the DE and ask if you can get a receipt for the costs of copying from your doctor, and be reimbursed for this expense by the DDS. This should be no problem. If the DE says there is no reimbursement, and you really need the money, this is the time to call the supervisor and speak about this with him.

Most often hospitals respond well to medical records requests. When they don't however, getting hospital records can sometimes be even more difficult than getting records from your doctor. Medical records clerks at large hospitals process requests non-stop all day long. Calling them and inquiring can be productive. There will be times, however, when you will have to demand a copy of your medical records from them like you may have had to do with your personal physicians. It can be a fight to obtain them and at times doctors and medical personnel will tell you that you can't have them or try to dissuade you from requesting them. They may say they were already sent or tell you to have the DDS request them again. All this has already been done or you would not be calling them.

You will have to be tough and insistent to get them to send you a copy of your records. You may want to pick up the records personally, since there has already been a delay in getting them mailed. Some HMOs are notorious for denying their patients access to their medical records. It is important that you understand that you have a legal right to your records. I can't tell you how tough this can be, but you must stand up to some incredible intimidation and demand your records. You may have to go up the chain of command here, as you're told it will take 60 days for them to get you a copy and other such misinformation to discourage you from following through. Be persistent, the implications for your life are long-term.

Even if your records are received by the DE, many times they are sketchy or do not contain the kinds of information that disability regulations require; they are insufficient and the DE is unable to make a decision based on these records alone. In these cases, the DE will order a Consultative Examination. This is an exam that the DDS pays for and it is usually performed by a doctor in the community who is willing to take the low fees that Social Security pays. Consultative examinations are also ordered for people who allege disability, but for any number of reasons, they have not seen a doctor recently.

For some medical specialties or if you live in a remote area, you may be required to travel some distance for the exam arranged by the DE. Generally speaking examinations are scheduled as close to the claimants home as possible. Sometimes, however, for various reasons, there is no doctor or hospital near the claimants home that can or will do the necessary exams or testing. In these cases you will be required to travel to the nearest doctor or facility where this can be done. Occasionally it is quite a distance. You can be reimbursed for travel expenses (ask the DE about this). A rare exception might be that you are unable travel due to the severity of your illness, but then this would have to be documented by a doctor.

It is more beneficial for you to have an examination by your own doctor if possible. The DE can authorize that your doctor receive the Consultative Examination fee and do the exam. If you have your own doctor and receive notification that you have a Consultative Examination scheduled, you should call the DE immediately and politely ask why the exam is required. It may be your records were never received at the DDS, or the DDS or postal service may have lost them. Your doctor may have failed to send your records or they may be insufficient. This is when you ask if you can have your own doctor do the exam. The DE should be able to arrange this for you. Be sure the DE supplies your doctor with a form that lists all the information needed. Everything regarding exams applies to MENTAL as well as physical exams.

Most doctors have no clue what Social Security regulations require. I say this based on the 100's of examination reports I've seen that were insufficient. Your doctor is concerned about your treatment; the DE needs a physical exam with very specific information. This information differs from one impairment to another. A stress test may be needed in a heart case, a medication blood level in a seizure disorder, a pulmonary function test in a lung illness, ranges of motion, reflexes and more in a musculoskeletal (bones and muscles) injury or illness. If the DE says there is no form for examinations, then ask the DE exactly what he needs and make a written list and take it to your doctor. **Also get an MSS form from the DE to take to your doctor to complete. REMEMBER: COPIES, COPIES, COPIES OF EVERYTHING.** Again, if the DE says he has no MSS form, ask him what specific information he needs, write it down and take it to your doctor at the exam. Normally there should be no problem getting these forms.

If you do not cover these two issues, an exam performed with all the information needed and an MSS provided with all the information needed, the exam will be much less valuable and probably insufficient. I have had to schedule an additional CE for claimants because the CE we got from the claimant's treating physician did not contain the information required. **Remember these two items :A complete examination that covers everything the DE needs; a complete MSS that also covers every point the DE requires.**

You should also be aware that it is easier for the DE to use a doctor other than your own for a CE. You will often encounter resistance from the DE to use your doctor for the CE, even though the regulations clearly indicate that the treating physician is to be used if at all possible. It takes extra paper work and arrangements for the DE to schedule with your own doctor. He may already have scheduled with one of the doctors on the CE panel (doctors in the community that SSA has contracted with). Now he will have to cancel the examination with a panel member, do a whole new set of paperwork and schedule an examination with your doctor. In addition, he already knows that most non-panel doctors don't provide all the information needed, nor do they usually provide it in the form in which he would like to see it. Again, you will have to be insistent and press the issue. **Find out first if your doctor is willing to do the examination.** Many doctors will not because the fee is too low or they do not want to render opinions about their own patients in case the claim is denied, thus risking having the patient blame them.

If you call the DE and argue for a treating physician CE and then find out that your doctor won't do it, you'll not only look foolish, but you may have slowed down the decision making process and delayed an outcome by as much as 60 days or more, depending on scheduling conflicts. Call the DE only after you have confirmed that your doctor is willing to do the exam, for the fee offered (which you have found out from the DE by calling and asking how much he will pay for the CE to be done by your own doctor). Also, you'll need to know how soon your doctor can do the examination. Two months out is usually not acceptable to a DE. Three or four weeks is more in the ball park, sooner if possible. This is a good time for me to give you a day in the life of a DE.

∗∗∗

Understanding the Disability Examiner

This description applies to California Examiners and comes from my own experience. I suspect that it is about the same from state to state, however, I have heard that in smaller states the workload is more reasonable. Typically a DE gets about 15 cases per week. That means he has about 2 hours to make a decision on each case when you factor in meetings and ongoing training. Of course, some cases are quickly disposed of, and more difficult claims take longer. The point here is that DEs are typically working as fast as they can to keep up with the load.

Each week every examiner's statistics are published for everyone in the branch office to see (in our branch there are over 150 people. It's like getting a report card every week). The statistics include how many cases the DE was able to complete, how many total cases are pending decisions, what the average length of time it takes him to complete a case is, and other such information. In addition, there are a number of cases that go for quality review at the local office level and also to the regional federal office. The pressure to perform is constant.

The task of the examiner is to keep up with the workload while doing quality work. In order for him to accomplish this, it is not unusual for DEs to skip breaks, take short lunches, and work overtime. Although discouraged by management, I've known Examiners who worked over 40 hours per week, without any overtime pay, to keep up.

DEs often do get overtime (a rarity in most State of California jobs), but usually they have to take extra cases to get the overtime. At my branch office a DE typically would take one extra case for every two hours of overtime offered. In extreme circumstances where work is really backed up there have been consecutive months when a DE could have virtually all the overtime he was willing or able to work. At one period our office was open 7 days a week, 6:00 AM to

8:00 PM including holidays. There is almost always more work than can be completed.

Typically a DE has a bachelor's degree or higher. Formal training is given for one full year, which includes classroom lectures by doctors and program experts. Some trainees are not able to do the work because of its complexity and the constant pressure to produce, and drop out during training; others drop out at the end of the one year probationary period. It takes about four years for a DE to become a journey level Examiner.

All this to say, the DE is extremely busy and working on complex issues where he is expected to make independent, timely, and accurate decisions. This I hope gives you a little insight into why the DE is sometimes abrupt and seems to be rushing you along. Much of what the claimant wants to tell the DE is irrelevant to the claim. Of course, the claimant is not at fault for not knowing this, but having this book should help you understand a little better what the DE needs. The DE needs **evidence** to make a determination on your claim. **Medical and lay evidence via all the ways we have mentioned above.** Let me reiterate that the Examiner you are contacting is overworked, pressured to move cases, pressured to do quality work, publicly scrutinized via weekly statistics, and has a type A personality (or he wouldn't still be working as a claims examiner). **Help him get the evidence he needs to** make a determination on your case and he will love you, take my word for it. His goal is roughly the same as yours, to complete your claim as accurately and quickly as possible.

CHAPTER 4

Medical Evidence; Disability Defined

Medical Evidence

The claimant is responsible for providing medical evidence to the DDS and DE. The DE requests the claimant's medical records from the treating sources listed on his application. As we noted above, however, the ultimate responsibility lies with the claimant to provide enough evidence for a determination to be made. The only acceptable evidence is that which comes from doctors, psychologists (licensed), optometrists for certain specified visual impairments, and licensed speech and language pathologists. Other types of health professionals records, such as chiropractors, physical therapists, and social workers are used as supporting evidence, but they cannot be the primary source used to establish a medically determinable impairment or its severity. Additional lay evidence like the Teacher Questionnaire, day-care worker reports and employer reports provide another type of collateral evidence that often is given great weight in the determination.

The **treating source** is the most important medical source because SSA has determined that the claimant's own doctor knows his own patient best and therefore SSA gives greatest weight to that evidence. The claimant's doctor also knows the medical history of his patient which is another important factor in determining how severe an illness is. This information though, must contain several elements to be complete.

Often a claimant will call me on the phone and say that their doctor said they were disabled. They then fax me a note that says something like, "Joe Smith is disabled due to arthritis." This is totally useless to the DE because SSA says it is unacceptable.

Here is a list of the needed items in a medical report from the book the DE uses to adjudicate claims, *Disability Evaluation Under Social Security* (it is referred to as the "Listings Book"):

• Medical history

• Clinical findings (such as the results of physical or mental status examinations)

• Laboratory findings (such as blood pressure, x-rays)

- Diagnosis

- Treatment prescribed with response and prognosis

- Medical Source Statement: a statement providing an opinion about what the claimant can still do despite his impairment(s), based on the medical source's findings on the above factors.

This would be a good list to take to your doctor to insure that complete information is provided. Often your doctor knows your condition well enough that he can prepare a complete report from his records and personal knowledge without even having to see the you again. More often though, a complete physical will be needed and the form from the DE should be used. This is the only way to insure that you will get what you need. **Remember, as has been stated above, a follow-up visit to your doctor last week does not constitute an examination. An examination has specific elements that it must contain. The form that the DDS and DE can supply is one way to insure complete evidence.** The DDS format is not required, and often medical evidence received is sufficient. Recommending the use of the DDS form is simply to help you maximize your chances of having a complete picture of your impairments presented to the DE. It also is a help to your doctor who most often will not know exactly what the DE needs.

✶✶✶

Disability Defined

Most claimants have no idea of what it means to be disabled under Social Security Disability rules. It is important to know that there are many kinds of disability programs, each with its own rules. Most people think that if they can no longer do the last job they worked at that they are disabled. Other claimants do not understand why they are disabled according to Worker's Compensation but not according to Social Security. Each program has its own definition of disability and as a general rule the strictest and most difficult definition is Social Security's. Part of the definition of SSA disability is the inability to work **any** job in the American economy. That means that even though you may unable to be a carpenter because your back is injured, if you can do less strenuous work, like sitting at a conveyor belt sorting socks, then you are not disabled according to SSA rules.

In addition, the disability must meet another requirement: it must be expected to last at least 12 continuous months or be expected to end in death. If you have a broken leg that keeps you from doing any work, but with treatment it is expected that you will be well in four months, then this does not meet the 12 month requirement. If the bone does not heal and you are unable to work for the required period, you will receive benefits back to the date your disability was determined to have begun. If on the other hand you were diagnosed with cancer one month ago and you are expected to only live a few months, then the 12 month duration is not an issue because your illness is expected to end in death.

Another condition that must be met is that the impairment must be a "medically determinable impairment." You cannot be considered disabled because you say you are disabled. The impairment must be diagnosed by an approved medical source and his diagnosis must be confirmed by the requirements for medical evidence that we mentioned above: Medical history, clinical findings, and laboratory findings. Some claimants allege an illness that has not been recognized by medical professionals, or have an illness that cannot be supported by any findings by a doctor. This will not be a medically determinable impairment.

Even if the impairment meets all the criteria above, it still must meet the test of severity. Many people have been diagnosed with illnesses, but they are not limited in any significant way, and thus are able to work. Claimants have told me that they are legally blind without their glasses. When

I ask them how they see with their glasses, they say I'm 20/20. There is no limitation here. Wearing glasses does not stop most of us from working. Another impairment that is mentioned often is high blood pressure. In most cases, unless the high blood pressure has damaged an internal organ severely, or it cannot be controlled at all with medication and is severely elevated, the condition is not limiting enough to be considered severe. Common allergies, run of the mill headaches, aches and pains of moderate severity and many other maladies we could mention are not severely limiting. These claims will be denied and the claimant will receive a letter that his illness is non-severe.

You must also realize that Social Security Disability is a functional program. One person may have severe degenerative arthritic changes on his x-rays, but is able to go for a two mile walk daily. Another claimant may have less severe x-ray findings, but is severely limited in his ability to walk. The function of the claimant determines his ability to work. I once had a claimant who had a broken bone in his leg that would not heal-it's called a non-union. The x-rays were clear that the bone had not knit. However, he played two hours of tennis everyday. He had no severe functional limitations. Yes, he had a medically determinable impairment, but it was clear there were many types of work he could do.

Even in severe illnesses, take Hepatitis C or HIV for instance, Many times a physical exam demonstrates that the individual is not severely limited in their ability to perform work activity. This is still called a non-severe impairment, not because it is not a severe illness, but because it does not place severe functional restrictions on the work activities of the claimant **at this time.** Benefits are not allowed on the basis of how ill the claimant may become in the future but on how the illness limits work activity today. At a future date the same impairment may be severe enough functionally to be considered disabling. That's why all denial notices contain language that if your condition worsens go to your local Social Security Office and reapply for disability benefits.

Disability then must be:

1. A medically determinable impairment.
2. Functionally limiting so that all work is precluded, except in the case of certain older workers, or those with certain educational, vocational, or language limitations.
3. Last at least 12 continuous months or be expected to end in death.
4. Remember, you may or may not be disabled because you are unable to perform your usual and customary work, that is the last job you worked for several years. Even if you have never worked, that does not preclude you from having the ability to work. Here we are back to a "case by case" evaluation, and the DE will have to factor in several medical and vocational factors in order to arrive at a determination.

CHAPTER 5

Denials and Cessations

I've been denied, now what? I used to get benefits, but now they have been stopped. What can I do? Reviewing your file. Reviewing your Consultative Examination.

Initial Claims

Denials:

At the time of this writing the process is being changed for the appeal processes for denied claims. Currently a denied claim can, at some offices, be eligible for a **reconsideration**. Reconsiderations are being phased out and replaced with the exit interview I mentioned above. It is impossible to say exactly what the final process will be. SSA is continually changing processes, regulations and procedures in an attempt to improve the system. In addition, congress sometimes changes the law and again this can change everything. Often these changes are triggered by law suits and in some cases U.S. Supreme Court decisions.

If you are notified that your claim has been denied (this will be by mail) and you have the right for a reconsideration, **you must go through this appeal step or you will have to begin all over again.** Applying for reconsideration is simple. Read your letter that is mailed to you from the DDS and make sure you meet the time-frames for a timely appeal. **Make sure you get the application form for the reconsideration from the CR/FO.** You must file by the deadline. Supply any new information: doctors you have seen, worsening of any conditions, any treatments done, any new illnesses you have. You are updating your original application. This information will go to a new DE and MC. Once the new evidence is received a new decision will be made and again you will be notified by mail.

If you are not eligible for a reconsideration you will instead be contacted that your claim is about to be denied and you have the opportunity to submit any additional information that you would like considered. This is the new process I am calling the Exit Interview. We went through that process in Part I, but essentially the difference is that you will provide the new information to the same DE and MC who are denying your claim, hoping that the new evidence will support an allowance. It appears the time-frames and deadlines on this process are shortened. A reconsideration had a 60 day deadline for filing the appeal application. The

Exit Interview may have a shorter time frame to respond and be provided the opportunity to present any other pertinent evidence or to make sure that all the evidence was received that you wanted considered for your claim. It will become increasingly important to read your mail carefully and look at the time limits that apply for an appeal. The current intent of SSA is to implement the exit interview method and delete the reconsideration level of review.

✳✳✳

I have been denied at my reconsideration or following my exit interview:

Whether by exit interview or reconsideration, a denial is a denial and the next step is the same. **Now you must apply for a hearing before an Administrative Law Judge (ALJ).** We have already indicated above that several months to a year or more is not an unusual amount of time for a case to wait to get a hearing before an ALJ. A word of encouragement here is that many denials are reversed at the ALJ hearing and benefits are granted back to the original date your disability began. Again, **you must go through this step of the appeal process**

or you will have to begin all over again. Look carefully at your letter of denial, call the FO and get the necessary forms to complete in order to appeal your decision. **Many** claims denied at the DDS are allowed by the ALJ. This is no secret, DEs tell claimants everyday on the telephone exactly what I am telling you here. In fact, nearly everything I've said so far is given to claimants by DEs, the problem is that they don't have time to give a complete picture like we're doing here. Most wish they did have the time to help the claimant more, but the time constraints and workload just prohibit that.

Likewise, Social Security is very concerned that claimants get a fair case decision and are informed of all their rights of appeal. There is no conspiracy to deny benefits to as many people as possible. The emphasis is on good decisions rendered as quickly as possible. If you have been involved in the system you may find this hard to believe, but it is the case. The rules for disability have been determined by the U.S. Congress and the DE must follow those rules. The Administrative Law Judge has more discretion, but SSA is working to bring the DDS and ALJ decisions to more closely conform to each other.

Some claimants get an attorney for the ALJ hearing. How to appeal is covered in the denial letter and SSA will provide you with a list of attorneys in your area who can help you. Some attorneys work on a contingency basis, that is if you do not win your case they collect nothing. Additionally, the amount they can collect is fixed by law. As I have stated in my disclaimer statement, I am not an attorney and cannot advise you on legal matters. Whether you get an attorney or not would probably be best decided by meeting with attorneys and discussing your case. Bring copies of all the records you have gathered. This is another good reason to pursue the tedious record keeping that I have recommended. The more documentation you have, the more an attorney or you yourself will have to work with to support your allegation of disability to the ALJ. **Again, give only copies of your records to attorneys or ALJs.** You may have to go further into the appeals process and you always want to have and control all the records you have gathered.

Before we leave the ALJ hearing, let me give you one very valuable piece of information. The ALJ hearing differs from the initial claim in one important detail: **The ALJ does not have to give you a second chance to attend an examination or provide any evidence he has requested of you.** The DE is constrained by certain regulations and must sometimes afford a second opportunity for claimants to do what is asked of them, for instance sending in a form, attending an exam, etc. The ALJ may just close and deny the case if you fail to do or provide something he has ordered. If you got several chances to complete items at the initial claim level, do not assume the judge will do the same; he doesn't have to and probably won't. The ALJ court calendars are backed up months and years. Miss something without a good and documentable cause and that's it: "Next Case!"

✷

My claim has been denied by the ALJ. Now what?

You will again be notified by mail. The next level of appeal is the Social Security Appeals Council. I've seen very few claims that had evidence that a claimant went this far with an appeal, but obviously some do. If you truly believe you are disabled then you have the right to do so, and should be encouraged to take advantage of the legal remedies you have.

If your claim is denied by the **Appeals Council**, you have the federal court system, beginning with federal district court, and continuing to the U.S. Supreme Court, in which to make your case.

✷

Continuing Disability Reviews (CDR)

I have been receiving benefits, but I have been notified that they are about to be discontinued or they have been stopped. Now what?

We are now addressing the issue of Continuing Disability Reviews, or CDRs. We did explain CDRs above, but there is more to know. First, every claim is reviewed periodically to make sure disability continues. This is routine. Some claimants call the DE frantically and ask if they have done something wrong? They wonder why they have been singled out for scrutiny. It is a regularly scheduled review, and all cases like yours go through the same process. Secondly, SSA (or the U.S. Congress) has purposely made it more difficult to cease benefits than to initially deny a claim.

In order for benefits to be ceased, the DE must be able to demonstrate that significant improvement has occurred and that the improvement is related to the ability to perform work related activities. SSA is not interested in seeing if there is some way benefits can be terminated; on the contrary, there must be conclusive evidence that significant improvement has occurred and that the claimant can now work. Again, the standard for work is not returning to your last job, or any job that you ever worked, but any job in the American economy.

An unskilled job that is sedentary would qualify; a job that can be learned in a five minute demonstration and requires only that you be able to sit and manipulate your hands for very light activities. The example we gave was sitting at a conveyor belt and sorting socks. This job would also allow you to alternate sitting and standing, which applies an even stricter standard.

Before any consideration concerning jobs though, the standard of improvement is applied to the medical impairment for which you were allowed. **Many claimants do not know what they were allowed for initially.** When you are notified that your claim is due for a review, call the FO, or if the claim is at the DDS call the DE, and ask what you were allowed for-that is, what are the specific illness(es) for which you were allowed disability benefits? You may be surprised that you were allowed for an illness you hadn't even considered or known about. Then you will follow all the steps outlined in Part I for an initial claim and especially try to document the severity of the illness for which you were initially allowed. Why? Because the DE must first show improvement in that initial impairment for which you were allowed before he can consider anything else. If there is no significant improvement then your benefits are continued for another period of time until due for the next review. If there is significant improvement, however, then the DE will consider other illnesses you may have had then, or that you have become ill with since your initial allowance.

Provide all the information you can to the DE. If you know that very little or no improvement has occurred or there has been worsening of your condition, there should be little to worry about. If you know that there has been quite a bit of improvement and you are able to do a lot more activity or your mental condition has improved and you can now concentrate and finish tasks, you can expect that a cessation may occur. That is, benefits will stop. There is an appeal process for this too, however, and benefits continue, if you wish, while the appeal is being made. Benefits are not discontinued for about 60 days, so if you appeal and desire benefits to continue during this period, usually there is no interruption of your payments. The best preventive medicine here though, is to take the reinvestigation of your claim seriously. and use all the tools in Part I to provide a full picture of your current state of health.

It may be the case, however, that you have developed new illnesses since you were first allowed. These new impairments must meet the standard of an initial claim. There is no standard of improvement because you were not allowed for the new impairments and there is no baseline function against which to compare the new functional limitations, if any. Any new allegations of disability then will be approached by the analyst as if they are being submitted as a new claim.

At the time of this writing (and I have heard nothing about changing this) a cessation of a claim, if appealed, receives a hearing at the DDS. The Hearings Officer is a specially trained journey Disability Examiner. He will schedule a hearing where you may appear in person and present evidence that your benefits should not be ceased. You can bring doctors or other witnesses or third parties that know your condition. In some cases the hearing may be done by telephone. **Be aware of the fact that the Hearings Officer need not give you several chances to comply with his requests for you to attend exams or provide evidence and questionnaires.** Therefore, when asked to do something by a Hearings Officer, comply fully and timely or your benefits may be ceased for noncooperation.

It is permissible, and probably prudent, to call the Hearings Officer prior to your hearing, and as with any DE, ask what you can do to help provide him with all the information he needs to make a determination on your case. Most DEs will be happy to let you know how you can make their job easier and provide evidence for an accurate and timely decision. But let me reiterate, **the Hearings Officer has powers similar to an ALJ with respect to being able to make an independent decision and offer you only one chance to comply with regulations.** If your claim is denied at the hearings level of appeal, and you believe that you are still unable to work, you should call the Hearings Officer or the FO and ask what the next step in the appeal process is.

All that we said above about medical records, mental and physical examinations, Medical Source Statements, questionnaires, etc. apply here. You want to have all the evidence you can at this hearing. And in case you are wondering if denials are ever reversed at hearings, the answer is yes.

Reviewing Your File

You have the right, after a decision is made, to look at your file at the FO. There are certain exceptions, for instance a review of your file reveals that it would be more appropriate for your representative to review your file due to certain sensitive issues. This could be a family member, friend, or whomever you designate. But generally speaking you will be able to look at your file personally. You need only call the FO and setup an appointment to do so. To my knowledge only a few claimants of the more than 4,000 for whom I have worked processing their claims have taken advantage of their right to review. Some who have though, have called me back to say that there is incorrect information in the file. I have no doubt that this occurs.

If I were a claimant, knowing what I do about claims adjudication, I would by all means review my file, and take whatever steps are appropriate and available to correct any errors. Some examples of errors have included wrong medical records used to make a determination because a person with the same or a similar name had records at the same facility; Social Security numbers are wrong; vocational and educational information is incorrect. Without going into great detail, please understand that your age, educational level attained, past work history, and ability to speak English are **very important factors in determining disability, especially if you are 50 years of age or older.** Verifying these items and all the facts in your file may result in a reversal of the decision or at the least will allow you the chance to correct inaccuracies so that your case is correct and the next reviewer will have the right evidence.

REMEMBER, THIS IS YOUR CLAIM. NO ONE CARES ABOUT YOU AS MUCH AS YOU DO. IT IS YOUR RESPONSIBILITY TO INSURE ACCURACY. IF YOU ARE IMPAIRED IT IS PROBABLY A GOOD IDEA TO FIND SOMEONE WHO CARES ABOUT YOU TO HELP YOU WITH A REVIEW.

✶✶✶

Reviewing Your Consultative Examination

From our previous discussion you may remember that a Consultative Examination is an exam ordered and paid for by SSA because there is insufficient medical evidence to make a determination. The exams may be for laboratory tests, psychiatric examinations, psychological testing, speech and language testing, hearing and eye tests, or any number of general or specialty medical exams. When you receive the notice to attend the examination there is a separate form that you return to the DE confirming that you will attend the exam and also to whom you would like a copy of the exam sent, usually a doctor. A copy will **not** be sent to you, but can be sent to your attorney or representative or doctor. If, however, you wish to see the results of the examination, it will be in your file at the FO and you should be able to see it after a decision has been made (see the section above on reviewing your file).

I would strongly advise reviewing this exam. At the DDS we do hear complaints concerning the examinations we order. The most common complaints are that the exam was so cursory in nature that it does not appear reasonable that the examiner could provide information regarding what work activities the claimant is able to perform. If you feel the examination you received was not adequate or you have other complaints, you may want to consider writing a letter indicating your concerns and having it placed in your file. Neither Social Security nor the DDS wants an examination that is inadequate. The examinations are paid for and are expected to meet commonly accepted medical standards. There is monitoring of complaints and efforts are made to get good examinations for the DDS/DE/MC to use to make decisions, but like everything else in life, the ideal is not always realized.

CHAPTER 6

Mental Disorders

Mental disorders, although requiring a different form of medical evidence, that is, psychiatric findings versus physical findings, still have the same general requirements for evidence that any other impairment does. A mental disorder must be a medically determinable impairment. That is it must be established by medical evidence consisting of signs, symptoms, laboratory and/or psychological test findings. The impairment must also meet the durational requirement of lasting one continuous year. In addition, a mental impairment must have a sufficient longitudinal history of the impairment that can be documented.

For a finding of disability due to mental illness, it is not enough to have a diagnosis of a psychiatric impairment. There must also be documentation of the degree of severity and the limitations caused by the impairment. For instance, not everyone who is depressed is unable to work. Many people with untreated depression work daily. In addition, there are many other depressed people who are successfully treated with medication so that they are able to work. The

Daily Activities Questionnaire, the third party Daily Activities Questionnaire, Employer Questionnaire, and other evidence that demonstrates the inability to function at a level that allows sustained work activity is crucial.

In today's medical climate many claimants are treated with medication for mental impairments by the primary care physician who is not a psychiatrist. While these records are helpful in establishing a longitudinal history of the impairment they are not usually sufficient to evaluate the severity of the impairment. A primary care physician who is not a psychiatrist (or a licensed clinical psychologist) cannot under SSA regulations diagnose or provide an examination, diagnosis, prognosis and other evidence that is sufficient to make a disability determination for a mental disorder. Often the DE will need to order a Psychiatric or Psychological Consultative Examination. Once a medically determinable impairment has been established, with a medical assessment of the severity, four areas of function must be assessed: Activities of Daily Living; Social Functioning; Concentration, Persistence and Pace; Deterioration or Decompensation in Work or Work-like Settings.

***

Activities of Daily Living:

This area, as the term indicates, is often assessed using the ADL questionnaire. Most claimants do not understand the importance of this form. They appear to approach it as so much busywork and formality. It is, however, as vital as medical evidence for the determination of a mental disability. In general, the form asks for a detailed description of what a claimant can do on a daily basis. For example, can the claimant do housework, pay his bills, take care of his own personal grooming, use public transportation or drive, use the telephone? This of course is just an example of the many activities that we do each day and that are assessed using the ADL form. Each of the activities of daily living is assessed according to the effectiveness of the activity with regard to the claimants ability to perform it independently and appropriately.

Is the claimant able to perform his ADLs with no help, a little help, or does he require much assistance and supervision? Does the claimant need assistance in getting to and from treatment due to his mental condition? Is the claimant able to do his ADLs without prompting or does he need continual reminders to change clothes, bathe, brush his teeth and so on? The total picture of the degree of impairment is assessed. There is no arbitrary number of activities that must be limited, but the overall effect of one or more limitations is judged by its limitations on the claimant's ability to perform work like activities.

What I would like you to take away from this discussion is the importance of all questionnaires, both first and third party, that you receive, or that are sent to others on your behalf. Do not treat them lightly; be complete and detailed. Call for help if you do not understand the questions. Get someone else involved. A social worker at your local social services office, a family member, the DE with specific questions.

✳✳✳

The second major area of evaluation is Social Functioning:

If a claimant is severely restricted in his ability to function with other people, this limits, but does not totally erode, his ability to work. For instance, there are jobs that require very little or no contact with the public, coworkers, or supervisors. A claimant with some social function impairment might still be able to do some type of work that exists in sufficient numbers in the American economy. An example of this might be planting seedlings in the forest. Gas and electric meter checkers also have less contact with people than some other jobs. Social function is, however, sometimes so impaired as to prevent any kind of work.

When we speak of social function we are talking about the ability to interact appropriately and communicate effectively with other people, as well as to get along with others. The questions on the ADL forms as well as the history and examination provided by the psychiatrist and psychologist should indicate where problems and limitations exist. In these instances, reports of third parties become critical. Can a neighbor supply information regarding hostility or withdrawal from interaction with others? Is there a police record of altercations, complaints and incarcerations? Are there others at stores, public agencies and other places, who can provide a description of the above?

Sometimes social functioning is characterized by such fear that a claimant is unable to function outside their home environment at all. This of course could so severely restrict the claimant's activity so as to preclude all work. Usually, however, it is a combination of limitations to some degree in one or more of all four areas that lead to a conclusion that a claimant is indeed mentally disabled to the degree that he is incapable of sustaining any work activity.

✶✶✶

The third major area of evaluation is Concentration, Persistence and Pace:

If a claimant is unable to focus and stay attentive to his work, he isn't going to last long on the job. Similarly, if he is unable to work fast enough, no employer is going to keep him. These same deficits can be seen around the home in the inability to follow a recipe, to finish mowing the lawn, or take out the trash without being sidetracked. Psychological testing is often the best way to measure the severity of these mental deficits. Often the DE first discovers these problems when he has gotten a mental status examination from a psychiatrist. It is not unusual to have to follow-up with testing. Employer questionnaires are helpful support evidence if available. Sometimes an employer will indicate that an employee had performed at an acceptable level for a period of time and then gradually his work deteriorated. He couldn't seem to complete a task. He began to have trouble following instructions. His work slowed down significantly. In cases of trauma or other kinds of illnesses and organic diseases the deterioration may be more sudden. This spills over into the fourth area of assessment.

***

Deterioration or Decompensation in Work or a Work-like Setting:

Simply put this is when a person breaks down or falls apart at work or in a work-like setting. The claimant is unable to take the stress of a job and either quits his job, or gets fired, and has developed symptoms so severe that they interfere with his ability to work. Impaired decision making, irregular attendance, inadequate interactions with other people, and inability to complete simple tasks, are just a few examples of deficits that might cause decompensation.

Afterword

I have tried to provide you with the information you need to present your case as fully and completely as possible. Each Disability Examiner approaches case development differently. If you see ways this book could be improved, or you have comments, please email me at ssimikedavis@aol.com. Unfortunately I cannot answer questions about your individual claim. I may be able to include information in subsequent editions if warranted. I wish you the best in your life and health.

About the Author

Mike Davis lives in Northern California and works for the State of California's Department of Rehabilitation. He is a contributing editor to Pacific Fisherman Magazine. Prior to his work in disability he was a minister for 14 years.

Appendix

Appendix A: The Disability Examiner

The Disability Examiner:

Name:

Address:

Telephone:

CONTACTS

Date   Subject

The Disability Examiner:

Name:

Address:

Telephone:

CONTACTS

Date   Subject

.

The Disability Examiner:

Name:

Address:

Telephone:

CONTACTS

Date   Subject

The Disability Examiner:

Name:

Address:

Telephone:

CONTACTS

Date   Subject

Appendix B: Field Office Information

Field Office:

Address:

Telephone:

Claims Representative:

Name:

CONTACTS

Date   Subject

Field Office:

Address:

Telephone:

Claims Representative:

Name:

CONTACTS

Date   Subject

Field Office:

Address:

Telephone:

Claims Representative:

Name:

CONTACTS

Date   Subject

Appendix C: Treating Source Information

Include all doctors, psychologists, hospitals, labs, physical therapists, teachers, social workers, day-care workers, counselors, and all others you would like to make sure are contacted for evidence and information to support your disability claim. You may wish to keep notes on contacts, if treating source responded to requests for evidence and records, and other important information.

Name:

Address:

Telephone:

Specialty, type of facility, or profession

Dates: First seen   Last seen

Treatment, medications, tests, surgeries, etc.

Notes:

Include all doctors, psychologists, hospitals, labs, physical therapists, teachers, social workers, day-care workers, counselors, and all others you would like to make sure are contacted for evidence and information to support your disability claim. You may wish to keep notes on contacts, if treating source responded to requests for evidence and records, and other important information.

Name:

Address:

Telephone:

Specialty, type of facility, or profession

Dates: First seen   Last seen

Treatment, medications, tests, surgeries, etc.

Notes:

Include all doctors, psychologists, hospitals, labs, physical therapists, teachers, social workers, day-care workers, counselors, and all others you would like to make sure are contacted for evidence and information to support your disability claim. You may wish to keep notes on contacts, if treating source responded to requests for evidence and records, and other important information.

Name:

Address:

Telephone:

Specialty, type of facility, or profession

Dates: First seen   Last seen

Treatment, medications, tests, surgeries, etc.

Notes:

Include all doctors, psychologists, hospitals, labs, physical therapists, teachers, social workers, day-care workers, counselors, and all others you would like to make sure are contacted for evidence and information to support your disability claim. You may wish to keep notes on contacts, if treating source responded to requests for evidence and records, and other important information.

Name:

Address:

Telephone:

Specialty, type of facility, or profession

Dates: First seen   Last seen

Treatment, medications, tests, surgeries, etc.

Notes:

Include all doctors, psychologists, hospitals, labs, physical therapists, teachers, social workers, day-care workers, counselors, and all others you would like to make sure are contacted for evidence and information to support your disability claim. You may wish to keep notes on contacts, if treating source responded to requests for evidence and records, and other important information.

Name:

Address:

Telephone:

Specialty, type of facility, or profession

Dates: First seen   Last seen

Treatment, medications, tests, surgeries, etc.

Notes:

Include all doctors, psychologists, hospitals, labs, physical therapists, teachers, social workers, day-care workers, counselors, and all others you would like to make sure are contacted for evidence and information to support your disability claim. You may wish to keep notes on contacts, if treating source responded to requests for evidence and records, and other important information.

Name:

Address:

Telephone:

Specialty, type of facility, or profession

Dates: First seen   Last seen

Treatment, medications, tests, surgeries, etc.

Notes:

Include all doctors, psychologists, hospitals, labs, physical therapists, teachers, social workers, day-care workers, counselors, and all others you would like to make sure are contacted for evidence and information to support your disability claim. You may wish to keep notes on contacts, if treating source responded to requests for evidence and records, and other important information.

Name:

Address:

Telephone:

Specialty, type of facility, or profession

Dates: First seen   Last seen

Treatment, medications, tests, surgeries, etc.

Notes:

Include all doctors, psychologists, hospitals, labs, physical therapists, teachers, social workers, day-care workers, counselors, and all others you would like to make sure are contacted for evidence and information to support your disability claim. You may wish to keep notes on contacts, if treating source responded to requests for evidence and records, and other important information.

Name:

Address:

Telephone:

Specialty, type of facility, or profession

Dates: First seen   Last seen

Treatment, medications, tests, surgeries, etc.

Notes:

Include all doctors, psychologists, hospitals, labs, physical therapists, teachers, social workers, day-care workers, counselors, and all others you would like to make sure are contacted for evidence and information to support your disability claim. You may wish to keep notes on contacts, if treating source responded to requests for evidence and records, and other important information.

Name:

Address:

Telephone:

Specialty, type of facility, or profession

Dates: First seen   Last seen

Treatment, medications, tests, surgeries, etc.

Notes:

Include all doctors, psychologists, hospitals, labs, physical therapists, teachers, social workers, day-care workers, counselors, and all others you would like to make sure are contacted for evidence and information to support your disability claim. You may wish to keep notes on contacts, if treating source responded to requests for evidence and records, and other important information.

Name:

Address:

Telephone:

Specialty, type of facility, or profession

Dates: First seen   Last seen

Treatment, medications, tests, surgeries, etc.

Notes:

Include all doctors, psychologists, hospitals, labs, physical therapists, teachers, social workers, day-care workers, counselors, and all others you would like to make sure are contacted for evidence and information to support your disability claim. You may wish to keep notes on contacts, if treating source responded to requests for evidence and records, and other important information.

Name:

Address:

Telephone:

Specialty, type of facility, or profession

Dates: First seen   Last seen

Treatment, medications, tests, surgeries, etc.

Notes:

Include all doctors, psychologists, hospitals, labs, physical therapists, teachers, social workers, day-care workers, counselors, and all others you would like to make sure are contacted for evidence and information to support your disability claim. You may wish to keep notes on contacts, if treating source responded to requests for evidence and records, and other important information.

Name:

Address:

Telephone:

Specialty, type of facility, or profession

Dates: First seen   Last seen

Treatment, medications, tests, surgeries, etc.

Notes:

Include all doctors, psychologists, hospitals, labs, physical therapists, teachers, social workers, day-care workers, counselors, and all others you would like to make sure are contacted for evidence and information to support your disability claim. You may wish to keep notes on contacts, if treating source responded to requests for evidence and records, and other important information.

Name:

Address:

Telephone:

Specialty, type of facility, or profession

Dates: First seen   Last seen

Treatment, medications, tests, surgeries, etc.

Notes:

Include all doctors, psychologists, hospitals, labs, physical therapists, teachers, social workers, day-care workers, counselors, and all others you would like to make sure are contacted for evidence and information to support your disability claim. You may wish to keep notes on contacts, if treating source responded to requests for evidence and records, and other important information.

Name:

Address:

Telephone:

Specialty, type of facility, or profession

Dates: First seen   Last seen

Treatment, medications, tests, surgeries, etc.

Notes:

Include all doctors, psychologists, hospitals, labs, physical therapists, teachers, social workers, day-care workers, counselors, and all others you would like to make sure are contacted for evidence and information to support your disability claim. You may wish to keep notes on contacts, if treating source responded to requests for evidence and records, and other important information.

Name:

Address:

Telephone:

Specialty, type of facility, or profession

Dates: First seen   Last seen

Treatment, medications, tests, surgeries, etc.

Notes:

Appendix D: Denial Record

Denial Record

Denial Date:

Reconsideration Filed?

Exit Interview?

Appeals:

Notes:

Denial Record

Denial Date:

Reconsideration Filed?

Exit Interview?

Appeals:

Notes:

Denial Record

Denial Date:

Reconsideration Filed?

Exit Interview?

Appeals:

Notes:

Denial Record

Denial Date:

Reconsideration Filed?

Exit Interview?

Appeals:

Notes:

Glossary

These definitions are not intended to be "bookish," dictionary definitions, or cluttered with medical terminology, but are, in abbreviated form, the kinds of explanations I would give a claimant over the telephone. Any further clarification can be gotten from the Disability Examiner at the Disability Determination Service where your case is being handled or from the Claim's Representative at the local Social Security Office where you filed your claim.

Generally speaking, all medical questions should be addressed to the DE and all administrative questions should go to the Field Office CR.

Activities of Daily Living: Normal day to day household activities such as cleaning, paying bills, personal grooming, using the telephone, etc. The Daily Activities Questionnaire (ADL) is most often used to assess these functions. By completing the ADL form carefully and completely all areas should be adequately covered.

Administrative Law Judge: A federal judge who makes administrative legal decisions. This is the person who hears the case at the first level of appeal for initial claims.

Appeal: Denied claims may be contested by the claimant. This process is called an appeal. All notifications of denial clearly state the rights of appeal available to the claimant. It is, therefore, very important to read any notices or mail received, and if not understood, to get help. Denial notices have telephone numbers included to call for information.

Body System: You may hear this terminology when talking with a DE. Often DEs use technical terms and abbreviations even when talking with claimants. Illnesses and impairments are classified by body systems. A heart problem is part of the Cardiovascular system, a seizure disorder is part of the Neurological system, and so on.

Claimant: Applicants who apply for disability are referred to as claimants by the DDS. Claims representatives at the local Social Security Office refer to claimants as "Number Holder's" or NHs, since they reference claimants via their Social Security Number.

Claims Representative: The federal employee at the local Social Security Office who takes the disability application and determines if all administrative requirements have been met.

Consultative Examination: This is a medical or psychological examination ordered by the Disability Examiner or in some cases by the Claims Representative due to insufficient or conflicting evidence in the claimants medical records. It may also include some kinds of specialty exams or laboratory tests.

Continuing Disability Review: A periodic review required by the U.S. Congress to assess the current medical and vocational status of claimants who are currently receiving disability benefits. Typically this occurs every three years, but can occur as early as six months or as infrequently as every seven years depending on the impairment. In practice some claims are not reviewed until much later than seven years due to the backlog of cases waiting for reviews.

Daily Activities Questionnaire: See Activities of Daily Living above.

Disability Determination Service: The state agency authorized by Social Security to make the medical determination regarding whether or not a claimant is disabled according to SSA regulations and standards.

Disability Evaluation Analyst: The name or classification given to Disability Examiners in the California state system of government. California handles more claims than any other state, and some of its local branches are larger than all the combined offices of some smaller states.

Disability Examiner: The state employee that makes the medical determination as to whether a claimant meets the Social Security standard for disability. The decision is made in consultation with a medical doctor or licensed psychologist.

Exit Interview: This is the term I have used to describe the new redesign process that Social Security is implementing nation wide. When a denial of disability is proposed, the claimant is notified and given the opportunity to present any new evidence he would like considered.

Federal Court System: The final step in the appeal process after all other remedies have been exhausted. Social Security and SSI disability denials may be appealed all the way to the United States Supreme Court.

Field Office: The local Social Security Office where a disability claim is filed. The Claims Representative works at this office.

Hearings Officer: A state employee who is a specially trained journey Disability Examiner that hears appeals on cases that had benefits ceased at the Continuing Disability Review due to significant medical improvement and current ability to work. These hearings are often held at the DDS or a local FO. The hearings officer, practically speaking, functions similar to a judge.

Initial Claim: The first time a claim is filed it is called an initial claim, as opposed to a claim which is being appealed, regardless of the level. CDRs, when reviewed are called initial CDRs as opposed to CDRs that are at some stage of appeal.

Lay Evidence: Evidence which is nonmedical, that is, evidence that is provided by a source other than a doctor, psychologist, or licensed speech pathologist, is considered lay evidence. This evidence cannot establish that an impairment is medically determined, but is important collateral evidence and can sometimes tip the balance in favor of the claimant. Examples are teachers, physical therapists, occupational therapists, school psychologists, employers, and other third party observers.

Listings (Book): You may hear the DE mention that the listings book requires certain evidence for your impairment. An example would be a laboratory test for rheumatoid arthritis, or range of movement for an injured back, or a blood level test of anti-seizure medications. The book also lists many very severe impairments that are automatic allowances if they *meet* all the criteria *listed.* This is the every-day handbook that the Disability Examiner and Medical Consultant use to see if the conditions for disability are met.

Medical Consultant: Each state has their own arrangement for using medical personnel in the decision making process at the DDS. In California, at the time of this writing, Medical Consultants are state employees. Each case is reviewed by a doctor to ensure that the analysts decision is correct. It is not uncommon for the Medical Consultant to make some changes on the proposed decision, which in almost every case the DE adopts in the final determination.

Medical Source Statement: We have gone into some detail in the text of the book regarding the MSS. Essentially it is the opinion of a licensed medical practitioner that details what, if any, limitations the claimant's impairments impose on his ability to perform work or work-like activities; or stated positively, what the claimant is able to do despite his impairments.

Number Holder: The claimant is referred to as the Number Holder, or NH, by the Claim's Representative at the FO, local Social Security Office.

Psychological Testing: Any testing done by a licensed psychologist. Other psychological testing may have been performed that is unacceptable because the person administering the test did not meet the criteria for a medically acceptable source. In other cases the testing is not acceptable because the specific test itself is not acceptable to SSA.

Questionnaires: Forms, usually sent out by the DE from the DDS, that cover a broad range of disability issues and vocational issues.

Reconsideration (Recon): Scheduled to be deleted in the disability process, the reconsideration is the first level of appeal after an initial claim is denied. Notification of the reconsideration process and deadlines comes with the written denial notice of an initial claim.

Social Security Administration: Refers to the Social Security Administration central office as opposed to the local and district offices that we have referred to as field offices.

Social Security Appeals Council: The final level of administrative appeal prior to initiating action in federal court. An appeal to an Administrative Law Judge would normally occur prior to a hearing before the Appeals Council.

Social Security Disability: Social Security Disability differs from SSI (Supplemental Security Income), but we have been using the terms interchangeably. Social Security Disability is authorized under Title II of the Act, and is applicable to claimants who have met the earnings and other administrative requirements for eligibility. Talk to a CR at the FO for further information. Note that the medical requirements for both SSA and SSI disability are the same.

Supplemental Function Form (Child): The equivalent of the ADL for children. This form is age specific and it is important that you read the title of the form to be sure it is for the age of your child.

Supplemental Security Income (SSI): Differs from SSA disability in administrative requirements only. The medical requirements for both programs of disability are the same. SSI, however, is intended to help claimants who are financially indigent as opposed to Social Security Disability which is awarded to those who have made payments into the Social Security System. The amount of monthly disability benefit payments made to a claimant may differ from that of SSA disability payments.

Third Party: Any person able to supply information about your condition. Many claimants are confused by the term third party. Essentially it means someone other than the claimant. For ADLs a family member or friend is acceptable. For the child's form, normally a parent or care-giver would complete it.

Treating Source: Any doctor or medical professional who has treated you. In the appendices for treating sources I have included teachers and other third party persons. They are technically not treating sources, but they are important sources of information and it seemed to make sense to have a record in one place rather than scattering them under many different titles.

Printed in the United States
25632LVS00002BA/310

9 780595 125746